Leabharlanna Poiblí Chathair Bhaile Átha Cliath
Dublin City Public Libraries

Dublin City
Baile Átha Cliath

Marino Branch
Brainse Marglann Mhuirine
Tel: 8336297

Date Due	Date Due	Date Due

Breaking Hearts and Traffic Lights

Patrick Chapman

salmonpoetry

Published in 2007 by
Salmon Poetry,
Cliffs of Moher, County Clare, Ireland
Website: www.salmonpoetry.com
email: info@salmonpoetry.com

ISBN 978-1-903392-64-5

Typesetting by Siobhán Hutson
Cover design and photography by Patrick Chapman

For lost loves

Acknowledgements

Grateful acknowledgements to the editors and producers of the following, where most of these poems appeared between 1994 and 2007, sometimes in earlier versions or in translation: *The Argotist Online, Argus, Astropoetica, At the End of the Day* (Anna Livia FM), *Carapace* (South Africa), *Cork Literary Review, De Brakke Hond* (Belgium), *The Dublin Quarterly, The Enchanted Way* (RTÉ Radio 1), *Eyewear, Fusebox* (Rattapallax, New York), Liberties College Radio, Lyric FM, *The Main Event* (RTÉ Radio 1), *nthposition, 100 Irish Poems of the Nineties* (Millennium 3 Press, Romania), *Poetry Ireland Review, Salmon: A Journey in Poetry 1981-2007* (Salmon Poetry, 2007), *Sunday Miscellany* (RTÉ Radio 1), *Sunday Miscellany: A Selection from 2004–2006* (New Island Books), *The Sunday Tribune—New Irish Writing, Trespass* (London), *Tribuna* (Romania), *Virtual Writer, W.P. Journal, Windows Poetry Broadsheet.*

Some of these poems appeared in two chapbooks from Lapwing, Belfast: *Touchpaper Star* (2004) and *Cicatrice* (2006). Some featured as part of *The Foot Series* art exhibitions and book (2001–2002), a collaboration with the artist Gemma Tipton. 'Your House' and 'Last Christmas by the Sea' were finalists in the 1995 *Sunday Tribune* Hennessy Literary Awards. Louise Jameson performed a version of 'Sea of Tranquillity' adapted for her by the author, on the CD, *The Actor Speaks 5: Louise Jameson* (MJTV, 2005).

Thanks to all at Salmon, and to the following, among others, for their close reading of the manuscript at various times: Djinn Gallagher, Roger McGough, Todd Swift and Gemma Tipton.

Many thanks to my friends and family for their encouragement, kindness, patience and inspiration.

Contents

Part Two

Part Three

Part Four

Part Five

Part One

Tiergarten Trilogy

Trees of the Tear Garden

In the last months of war,
Starving Berliners
Would chop down for firewood
Trees that had endured
The constant bombardment.

Now, the trees are numbered.

Between lanes lit by lamp posts
From towns the world over,
The ones that survived
Stand a little taller
Than the post-war plantation.

Kaiser Wilhelm Memorial Church

In flux on Budapesterstrasse,
Beside Kaiser Wilhelm's
—The roof still agape—
I see through the bomb damage:
Sky of a bomber.

Black birds are perching on jags
Like the reincarnations of airmen.

Memory Safari

It is forbidden to photograph the animals.
I snap a red deer. I freeze a flamingo.

I hunt for the elephant picture
Promised to the friend
Who had lent me her camera.

As evening falls, I sit on a bench
And watch the Zoo station across from the Zoo.

The Pentax is trained to detect any sign
Of the lover I'm here to forget.

Pith-Helmet Report

One night, when you needed him,
A man in a safari suit
Appeared in the room
Where you were sewing the triangles
Of a quilt that would take years.

You saw the space that he had filled,
The wisp of his dead breath.

An explorer who had brought
A Rosetta stone to decode
Your language of contentment,
He was the spirit of someone
Who used to live in this house.

His life, like a bullet, had passed
Long before you heard the report.

Mnemonic Set

The milk jug, sugar bowl, pottery mugs
That you stole for me in a restaurant
After a calendar shoot
—You'd have taken the tea pot
If someone had not
Been imbibing hash tea—
Recall early days
Cocooned in your flat:

We light a fire,
Swig gin from the naggin,
Exchange confidences,
Make love in a chair
And later, like kids,
Watch each other, surprised,
Take a leak.

Summer of Love, Vol. 1

Their first weekend, he loaded the stereo with batteries
And tilted it on the back seat. While she drove,
They played a selection of music cassettes:
Ella Fitzgerald, Marianne Faithfull, a trove
Of golden oldie records. Melanie sings
The Rolling Stones. Mama Cass is dreaming.

She took them west in her old car
Past Edgeworthstown where she'd been born,
Through Longford where her parents ran
A guest house. On to Oughterard, for
Painted candles from De Lacey's.

How privileged he felt, to be with her,
Downing warm Guinness in Naughton's,
Counting strange sea shells washed up on the shore,
Taking the salt of the incoming air
Like seasoning on their kisses, tongues
Bunched up in their mouths like molluscs.

Hotel International

This hotel with its vast marble walls
And indolent receptionist
Appears to be the perfect place to land.

We are off the plane, a charter called Excalibur;
Through the airport, shed with shop and landing strip;
Off the tram, its rickety chassis rattling downhill to the city.

We are here
On our first night together in a foreign country,
Where we can be different.
I am strong, for instance. I am open.

We have brought Jack Daniel's,
Fearful of a shortage in this *terra incognito.*

We have brought our bodies too,
And the first delicious pangs
Of this immense infatuation
That finds hotel rooms amazing.

Out the window is the night. It rains.
The lights of Prague seem distant.
We don't yet see the TV tower,
The Old Town Square, the details—but,
Unknown, this place holds dreams for us.

The tumblers on the table with its lampshade and its ashtray
Will now serve for our Jack Daniel's and tomorrow, for our
    toothbrush—
So we open up the alcohol. The night begins, with camera.

First Christmas by the Sea

Snow fell, layered on the house.
Inside, the two were celebrating
Six whole months of happiness.

Their Christmas goose was cooking
In the oven while they sat, undressed
—With no pretence to speak of—
In front of yuletide television:
Moira Shearer dancing. They
Admired her dress, the Technicolor.
Soon, they were embracing.

They began to flirt with
Recklessness—but paused to take
Precautions. Frame by frame,
The Red Shoes rolled.

Some time later, checking
That the weather was improving,
They had dinner, pulled a cracker.

In the small hours, after wine, warm hearth and sleep,
They woke to find the television on.
Somehow, snow had got inside the house.

Touchpaper Star

We stand back, watch the rocket rise
Too briefly in a night-sky arc.
It bursts into a globe of stars
That expands away from us,
Contracts towards the park.

In this way, we create dimension.

'Light the match.' In moments
The explosion has forgotten us.
It wonders how it came to be;
Invents a system of belief;
Evolves into a pall of smoke
While we go on demanding
Other universes. 'Quickly, strike—
While we still have the matches.'

Cochineal

You are buttering the bodies
Of insects on your knife,
Spreading them on stretched canvas,
Making wild symmetry,
Sudden geometry—
Resulting in a subtlety
At odds with the method,
Abstracts in which, like Rorschachs,
I could see whatever I wanted to see.

Once you painted me
But used a finer hand:
My head against tall window frame,
The sill like a harpoon.

Lovers

One summer morning when sciatic pain
Detained me, complaining, in bed,
You rose before clock-shrill,
Pulled socks on my feet,
Slipped pants over bristling skin.

You brought me my pill and a tumbler of water
Then sat me up gingerly, testing the spasms
That marked out the bounds of my movement.

You might have been fixing the pose of a dummy
Through which to project your new voice
But I did not appear to be wounded
Until after my nerve had returned.

Realty

This home that we are viewing
Is a state-of-the-union address:
One night, someone on the street
Might see the television light

Flickering on the ceiling
Like a very slow kaleidoscope

—Jewels of coloured glass
That once were fabulous—

And hope
That whoever may be living
Here can see in black-and-white.

Communication

In their bathroom with a rusty blade,
I tease myself with death.
It's no reflection on their hospitality.

I come downstairs.
The host ignites sambuca.
My lover, you're a ticking bomb of pleasure.

Later, home in bed, I hide
My coarsened wrist from you.
You do not see the graze.
We make love in the dark.

Eight Flights

I miss
Our post-osculatory somnolence—
Remembering one
Night in particular
When I had become a conductor of fear.

The knowledge
That your body earthed mine
Kept me from the window ledge.

Nocturnes

I

We are lying in the bed
That we had bought together,
Broken beam supported
By a tea tin full of coppers.

You are sleeping, in a dressing gown,
Curled up beneath your quilt. I fear
That if I draw it down,
You will have disappeared,
Leaving the impression
Of your contours in the cotton.

II

We used to make love in this bed,
No one to hear us but rodents
Propagating their kind, in the attic.

Now, we discuss feline mating.
Out on the wall by the mill,
A tom slams his dick in a cat,
Her pain when he yanks it away
Provoking the wailing
We hear through the window.

Nocturne

In tableau, we resemble
Two people in an accident,
My five-feet-ten stretched out
Alongside your spread-eagled body
In the wreckage of this bed
On which, come morning, we will wake
In the recovery position.

Morning, I revive you with a c.c. of saliva—
Lips applied with tenderness to lashes,
Lids behind which dreams
Are being put away for now,
Without interpretation
Or the dangerous enquiry:
'How are we doing, today?'

Cobain

You had driven west to put geography
Between yourself and my bleak humours. I
Was stunned by news, received in solitude:
Cobain had pulled a trigger on himself,
The pills and whiskey incident, a dress rehearsal rag.

Now, his wife and daughter desolate,
His mother had proclaimed her son
A member of that stupid club.

I'd only known his music, but I'd heard
His double-barrelled blow inside my skull
As morning light rays, April-harsh,
Attempted trepanation on my head,
To disperse the airs that seeped into my lobes
And threatened bad-demeanour meningitis.

I announced it to the first poor soul I found,
A shop hand who stared, innocently blank,
His digits probed by the checkout laser beam.

That night, as black-clad teenage acolytes
Congregated at the cross in Phoenix Park,
I kept internal vigil for a love
That, limping, had been put to sleep like some
Lame horse who faced the hypodermic and
The pasture of the dark: a kind of virtual
Euthanasia. We had buried it still breathing.

Suddenly, the world had flattened
Wide without a *Rough Guide* to the heart,
An atlas of the spinal cord,
A route map of the nervous system.

Marina

Here on the edge of the land,
I see that you've become half-mermaid
And must soon exchange your feet for fins,
And trade your pudenda for scales—
But keep your nipples to express
Mammal's milk to baby whales.

Breakers

I

Donegal getaway. Pixel-dazed, moping,
I holed up alone typing up my old novel
While you ventured out, doing holiday things:
Casing the beach, enjoying dips at dawn,
Photographing bladderwrack—as if
Preparing for waves to break over our heads.

II

Water will erode the land. An image of corrasion
Dogged me. I'd not join you in the sea
To share your parting of the waves and,
Having parted, trust the seabed, so
You took a stick, engraved my name in sand.
That excavated beach. I thought of moonscape.

III

One winter weekend when we are both old
We might walk from opposing directions,
Converge on the love-letter beach of our youth,
Our walking sticks now making broken-line tracks
That both follow and lead our old footprints
Down to the rim of a darkening sea.

The Whispering Wall

All day long you have been quiet.
The rushes by the road have made more sound
As wind soughs through the space between
Like breath upon an instrument:
A trombone for the soundproofed
Or a flute for the impaired.

You're reading Janet Frame in bed,
A broken-backed *Orlando* on the floor.
You turn a page. You do not speak.
I do not ask.

I want you to take up a pen
And scribble on the bedsheet:

Do not make me part my lips.
I've trapped a kiss inside my head
And dare not risk its flying out
Till I can pass it on.

But you're engrossed.

I slip into the living room. Outside:
A couple, leaving, handing back their
Late-November bolthole to its owner.

In an hour or two, a new pair will have come.
The walls of their vacation home
Will whisper nothing of the lovers just departed.

Last Christmas by the Sea

No pearl. I launched an oyster
Down the slipway of my throat.
In its wake a new Atlantic:
Guinness in a Roundstone pub.

Later, playing twenty-five,
Startled at my winning streak,
You semaphored: *Your round*,
Denied admission to defeat.

This will be the memory:
Midnight road with no street light.
We lay down in the puddles
And made out, in the Milky Way,
The six remaining Pleiades, one
Daughter lost in Taurus, stars
By which we could not navigate.

Your House

Visiting, I wash familiar dishes.
You make some tea and sweep the floor.

It is natural to do these things
And yet,
When we sit down together
You just as soon get up
To telephone your parents,
Turn the television on.

We channel-surf through silent
Dialogue of body language.

Time for me to go.

Outside, I take the wrong road home,
Lost in your new neighbourhood.

Banns

You will marry your man on an African beach,
The minister booked, your parents informed,
Your silver dress bought.

Now, the bridal bouquet's
Still a far-flung plantation of seeds—
But I can imagine your long limousine

Taking the sun like a veil on the chrome,
You and your man in the warm leather seat,
As the season of goodwill approaches:

Stone-splitting there, the usual hoarfrost up here
Where tinsel is hung on the neck of the tree
Like a noose killing off the old year.

When you return in the spring of the new,
Your conjugal bliss will insist on its place
In a world that is altered.

Hope of Ray

Thirty-six months to the day since we split,
In my sea-facing flat, the shower is blocked
With the hair of a woman not you, but herself—
And I love that long tangle of strands I pulled out.

This morning, she's resting. The comet's asleep
But the sun is awake. I am sprinkling boiled eggs
With black pepper, ground up. I am toasting
McCambridge's stone-wheat brown bread.

Later today we will go window shopping.
Tomorrow we might take a stroll on the beach
Or head for the cinema, there in the dark
Watching other lives spin their tales out.

Easter Comet

In New York you had contracted poison ivy.
Undeterred, you wandered Broadway in a night-dress.

This image of you, fearless of the muggers, jugglers, yuppie scumbags,
Comes to me tonight as I stare, standing on my front step,
Up at Hale-Bopp in the northern sky:

A portent of the plague in other ages, but in this,
An imperfection in the firmament,
Across from what is now a bloated moon
That runs fat rays into the clouds
And seems to call: 'My jaundiced skin!'
As though the sky has run off with some luminous new stranger.

Those clouds will drift and scatter over your side of the city
Till some hour of the morning when the sky begins to lighten. Now
The tide is rolling out. The sea goes on into the dark
Beyond lighthouses.

Part Two

In Recess: Requiescat in Pace

To Caroline

Prologue

Talk, as I and friends from Belfast
Celebrated in a Skreen Road house,
Was of a World Cup game and little else—
But, ten that night, Sky News cut in:

'Six mown down in Loughinisland
Overshadowed Eire's win—'

An out-of-season 'Trick or treat!'
Called out rounds in a public house,
A whole half day and more
Before your parents started back.

Sunday passed with hangovers,
A trip to Mother Redcap's.

You had said you'd phone on Monday
Morning. Anna Riordan called:
Your father and your mother in a car crash in Recess.

The Incident

The driver of the other car
                              The fire brigade cutting equipment
The passengers
                              Saved your mother for the ambulance
Your father
                                   But she was dead on arrival

So said the reports; and in the *Star*,
I saw a colour photograph: the cars
—Honda Civic, Ford Sierra—
Crushed like empty foil wrap.

You had woken to the doorstepping
Of news hounds on the scent of blood:
The *Evening Press* was staking out
Your family home at dawn;
The radio had broadcast names
Before the youngest son had heard.

Wake

In the hallway, grown men shook.
You took frail hands into your own.

In the garden, people meeting
For the first time in how ever long
Continued to pose
Questions begun on the phone.

Removal to the Sacred Heart

The priest praised their success
In business as in family—twin
Accomplishments of those on whom
The Church confers its grace—
His words on the public address
Like a broadcast from beyond, although
The coffins were still on their gurneys.

Moments from now, they will be raised
On the shoulders of those who have loved them,
Of those who will carry them out.

Shanganagh Cemetery

As we lined the drive inside the gates,
Awaiting two Fanagan hearses:
Another funeral.

We watched a small procession
Follow a black Mercedes
In the back seat of which,
Two men in dark suits
Rested across their laps
The white coffin of a child.

Loss Chant

The world is passing into recess.
    Love is always passing into grief.
Grief is always passing into morning.
    Morning, always passing into day.
Day is always passing into evening.
    Evening, always passing into night.
Night is always passing into morning.
    Morning, always passing into day.
Day is always passing into evening.
    Evening, always passing into night.
Night is always passing into morning.

Redemption

On a dresser in your home I see a photograph:
Four children ranked beside the two
Whose faces I expect to fade
By silver nitrate exorcism
In a horror film:

The voodoo has been made.
The stricken are not saved.

And I can have no faith
Or offer comfort but to say
That after life, their particles are free
To form a new relationship with nature—

Photons and electrons making
Nuclear dances with the earth,
Deeper than the sex that made you live:

Her atoms will connect with his.
His atoms will connect with hers.

Redemption in a law of physics:

Energy can never be created or destroyed.
It can only be transformed.

Part Three

Planet Virgo Collage

'I am not an underpant-wearer,'
You said before I guessed it and you proved it.

We were together a long time in dog years.

'Your voice is telling me you'll be sleeping in the wrong place.'

Beauty sweat will urge the petals.

'Fear not, little boy,' you warned.

Every day, you paint your shell,
A time-wrecked easter egg.

'Remember who you are, not who I want you to be.'

Teach me how to drink
As it is done in your mouth.

'Are you in love with me
Or with the strangeness, the exotic?'

Eat the sea.

'Adventure Central on Planet Virgo?
I just wanted to hear your voice.'

'You only want me for my brain.'

While you're using it, your vibrator leaks acid.
'I'm so hot I made the battery come.'

Womanlazygorgeous.

'Your eccentric personality has its charms
But isn't what a woman wants.'

Drive to power place,
Blue black water,
Essential bed man and I together.

You dance unselfconsciously, boasting:
'This is as close as we get to an orgy in public.'

    Take me with my haircut passing
    Lightly through the wetness of your lips.

Reading Annie Dillard. The female
Mantis bites the head off the male.
The brain in his ass
Is now free to fuck her.

    Like Grenouille, you want to hide
    In a cave for seven years.

Using my brain as a compass,
I discover your zones,
But am rumbled,
Smuggling my fingers through Customs.

    Phone sex across an ocean:
    Bondage of telephone lines and hot breath.
    You come, fall asleep and I can not hang up.

We've hardly said goodbye a week when you
Suggest I might donate my sperm.
'Who better to ask than a friend?'

    Some heave tiny men
    Above death and worship.

One day, you'll come home to find that
All the ghosts have moved out of your head.
You'll not know where to sit.

    'Hold your tongue so I can kiss your throat.'

Mecca Faces Us

Careless, we kissed in the court of a mosque.
The man who ran over to scold us and warn,
Pulled us apart before others could see.

Deaf to your pleas and our incomprehension,
He took us for ignorant Yankees,
Said we were lucky that we had not died
On the spot, of some lightning from God.

You took his sincere imprecations to heart,
Perceived no coincidence here.

Your husband, a stranger, knew nothing of this
But someone had fingered your collar,
Some Great Universal Policeman.
We shuffled outside in the rain.

There, I'd have jumped in the Seine to retrieve it,
Should you have thrown in the cold wedding ring
That your silversmith husband had beaten.

Shepherd Moons

A pair of bonsai asteroids: we picked
The limestone rocks up in the Burren,
Carried them back to the car, a hired
Fiesta—gleaming purple curves and glass—

A spacecraft in the wilderness,
Discordant with the fractal coast,
The hills of time through which we'd come,
Smiling at the words of our new song.

You stopped the car and nuzzled me.
The setting sun washed everything in gold.
The moment passed. We were in love.

Now, the rocks are on my mantelpiece,
A pair of shepherd moons without
A planetary ring to keep in line.

In Camera

Rifling through some old effects,
I found your head-scarf, wrinkled silk,
A courier of complexes.

Your chosen scent, patchouli oil;
A tincture of your skin's own sweat;
A touch of mine embedded in the layers:

The odours we distilled one night—
Hotel du Marais, five floors up—
As Paris wound around us like an iris.

The room zoomed in to frame you
As you wrapped the scarf about my cock—
A focus pull as you closed in.

The mirror-silvered ceiling screened
A pair of body doubles, stand-ins,
Siamese automata, connected at the hips.

Missing

You missed the park today. A mist rolled on
The bay and rubbed out the horizon. Howth
Dissolved and through the haze, a fog
Horn gave great voice, Leviathan about
To speak in public. As I sat to read
A page in Dillard—living in the now—

The mist began to lift, revealing mothers
Playing with their kids. A Malinois
Ran in the grass. A couple on the fractured
Pathway wandered hand in hand. The trees
Were hung with instruments: twenty kinds
Of whistleblower bird, concatenated.

If you were here, a dead crow in your jaw,
You would distinguish between all of them
And name their maker, name their songs. You'd know
The secret word of trees, the stranger Shepherd,
Flower buds. You'd know how to address the mist.
Come back and let me take your lead.

Trash

The dumpster lid is open.
As you empty out your trash can,
You hear scratching.

A night-obscured raccoon leaps out
And: *What the fuck is this?* you think.
Some animal is squatting in my—

Next time you'll remember that
Raccoons live in the garbage here
As city growth encroaches. You
Will check there's nothing live down there

Before you spill your coffee grounds,
Martini dregs, zucchini peel,
Used rubbers, eggshells, vermiculture,
Watermelon longitude.

Labyrinth

'I've taken all the vodka and the wheat beers are all gone.
    The pills are working, tiny fogs.'

'I guess I will be leaving here, this curious fall night.
    Got anything to say before I go?'

★

You could have left a thread for neutered Theseus to follow but—
    That night you were both Ariadne and the Minotaur.

Windows on the World

High above a passing bird, I sank a Gibson cocktail. I was
Bloodless from a perforated heart and wanted something
To replace the squandered fluid; felt the lure of mental illness; just

The other side of that too-solid window, I could catapult—but
Madness seemed like tiger balm, despair like acupuncture, so
I watched the evening terminator trailing blinking lights along

The night-devouring island to the twilight-loving Park. Up here,
My local drinking buddy, getting over someone too, was drawing
Street plans on a napkin. She was down there in those canyons,

He said, breaking hearts and traffic lights, accepting serenades
From stunned New Yorkers and their girlfriends. Then, I think we
Drank a toast to her, and raised a glass in praise of feeling low.

Desireland

I

The island is closed now to summer
Seekers after roots and hints of autumn,
Gatherers of archetypal facts.
John Ford's film plays daily
To an audience of ghosts.

The dying tongue is spoken here:
First language, and a barrier
Between the island and the world.
Hidden pubs are random beacons.

II

Night. The final fishing boat this century pulls in.
No more will be caught until
The sun comes up on New Year's Day.

Striking out along the coast,
I see slow-motion fireworks
That carry strangers back home to the Bronx
Or Galway. Then, a blackout—

Cloud and sea are cloven.
In that moment, I imagine this:
Your lubricated fingers,
Slipping the horizon's lips apart.

What We Leave Behind

Corona-backlit ruin on a hill:
O'Malley's ancient home.

In your lifetime, you're a pirate queen
But each succeeding generation
Dissipates your glory until—

Buried in the commerce of the world,
Your smile crops up, unrecognised.

Post-Mortem

I see you on a mortuary slab,
Your blue body bloated.

They've fished you out of the river Don,
Removed your clothes and wrapped you in a sheet.

There is no doubt it's you. There are a thousand
Men out there who could identify your body.

Your hair crowns a high forehead.
Below, a frozen smile—

You are daring the pathologist
To join you in a cold embrace

So that the moment he has gone,
You can feel abandoned.

Then you'll tell me how it was,
How he wouldn't come inside you,

But preferred to spill his seed
Between your breasts,

And how his ribcage was so thick
You could not reach his heart,

And how, when you said 'love',
He ran, refused to take your calls,

And came back in the morning
With his scalpel and his speculum.

I Loved You Here

It made him smile, her face when it returned
Without her body or the bottom of her chin.

You can burn and tear and throw them in the trash,
She told him then, but some will not stay dead.

He'd snapped one day a year before;
Removed what she had left behind.

The postcard—Horst P. Horst—
That she had hidden in his pillowcase:
I loved you here, in eyebrow pencil, cursive on the back;
The woman in her corsetry, unbound.

He balled her letters, burnt the lock
Of hair she'd mailed to compensate
For lack of her. The smoke became her ghost.

Her emails, he erased for all their suicidal tenderness
And casual demands
For neat shampoo you could not get abroad.

He threw away the books she'd given:
Walker Percy, Annie Dillard, H.R. Giger, James Agee—
Her taste had been impeccable and probably still was.

He found a note inside the fridge.
I loved you here or hereabouts—
The kitchen at whose table they had dined
On one another. He discarded all discovered relics
But her silken head-scarf that he'd accidentally
Laundered so it held her scent no longer.

Then, the photographs. The ones in frames he left
Until he'd burnt the others in their pockets,
Quickly, without looking—dropping them aflame
Into a cooking pot and slapping down the lid;
Switching off the mains in case the fire alarm
Would carry their death-wail upon the air—
And when their wisps had been absorbed,
He let the ashes sail into the street.

He took her portraits from the walls and stuck
A breadknife in their backs and prised the pictures out.
He stuffed the frames into the bin.
He made confetti of the prints.

One year on, her face came back, or part of it.
He smiled as though he'd recently learned how,
The use of his lips almost fully restored,
As after a long-ago crash.

Now, the pictures he'd destroyed were in his head.
He was the frame. For all of those sections of time
That contained a mere segment of her face, he had
Never captured her, had never understood that it
Takes two to make a photograph; that the shooter
Must focus on another, lest he look into himself
And recognise the image he's become.

Sunlit in the Burren with a purple car behind her—
    I loved you here.

Wearing his green woollen jumper in Paris—
    I loved you here.

Holding her nose as they forded at Ha'penny Bridge—
    I loved you here.

Part Four

Moon Sea Time

Some irregular night hour. The moon, anaemic, low-slung
In the tide of tissue-cumulus soft-circulating
Upwards toward an atmosphere dissolve. I take my instruments—
A pair of black binoculars and camera—outdoors to the sky: a star
Field trip, over to the barrier that breaks the Irish sea before
It's able to ingest the terraced houses in small increments.

I think of your low white-corpuscle count—the doctor
Told you yesterday—while up there hangs the moon,
Not running red, as in some prophecy of death,
But ashen-faced, its craters clear as to an
Astronaut in orbit of its changeless body; smaller, though,
As fits a man who's never left the Earth.

They say that when our time is gone, when every human
Being has evolved into some other form, and when
The Earth itself has died, and when the moon
Awaits that final flare of nuclear fire—as the solar system
Gasps expiring breath; they say what will remain
Of us are footprints in the lunar dust, without a sea to swallow them.

Cinderella Suffragette

She'd dreamt it: at the water's edge,
A glass shoe horned with one red rose

Not withered as it ought to have been; fairer
Than they would have deemed appropriate

Mere hours before, when she had been
Denied her chance to join the town's elite

And dance the ashes from her brow—
Upsetting their predictions

Of a future lived in shadow,
A mantle she could never shake,

A life defined the moment
After every lick of flame had died.

So, breaking out one night,
She burned her charred brassiere

And took her ashen body to the sea.
There, along the waterline,

She found the glass again, the rose
A prickly tongue inside; the moon,

Its obverse mirroring her face.
She tried the slipper on. It fit—

And being in need of none,
She sought no prince.

Mercy Fuck

What once was a charm
Is a relic now,
The bone of a saint,
Paraded for the curiosity of strangers
Who can never feel the holiness
But still expect the blessing.

We are dead.
We are dead.

Everything we are
Is a flame
Lost in the furnace
Of time.

I do not care
What we do tonight.
Come here to me. Come here.

Covetous Foetus

I want your life. I want
Your car. I want your
Job.

I want your joy in waking up
Each morning with my mother.

I want your smile.
I want to know
What it felt like
To make me.

I want to get drunk.
I want to take drugs.
I want breast milk laced with cyanide.

I want to jump off
The spire of the Duomo
To fall on sunbathers
On rooftop patios below.

I want a sunset on another world.
I want to take her breasts away from you.
I want an abortion.

Spiders

The spiders came from nowhere, spiralling out
Beyond the edge of an under-printed
Chinese take-out flyer in the hall: negative stars
In a transient anti-horoscope.

Later, they were gone. I thought
A neighbour had dispatched them with a pan,
But maybe they had crawled up to the capital,
Enrolled in Spider College, reading: *Engineering 101,*
Parachuting for Beginners, Architecture of the Web,
Intimate Geometry, Unpopular Mechanics—

And got on very well. I think they discovered
A coven of gigantic ants, practicing a magic
Ineffective against venom, spinner, silk. And now,
On summer nights, when I am going down on some
Found Art In A Black Dress, I imagine that the spiders spy,
Scrawling notes on what to do if they should meet a fly.

Sea Of Tranquillity

He came home from the party.
In his pocket was the satin star
He'd plucked from decorations.

He woke his daughter, not yet four years old.
He took her, drowsing, out into the road.

He pointed at the sky: the gap
Between Orion's shoulder blades.

'You see that space above the clouds?
I got a great long ladder, laid
The top rung on the moon,
And caught this star that now I give to you.'

Music Downstairs

Songbirds are long gone. The day is old.
I lie awake and naked in your bed.
You go downstairs to put the kettle on.

Instead you are diverted by the Steinway
In the living room. You never moved it when
You moved away from here, your parents' home.

And now—
The trickle of a Chopin polka
Rises like a rainstorm in reverse.

Later, over tea, you tell me:
Teachers never heard the music,
Just the notes you missed. It made you

Hesitant about your gift.
You put it down an age ago,
An age at which you could have gone
To Moscow.

The Party

Tomorrow, in the morning, late,
You will come down from his bedroom.

You will catch me snoring on the couch,
Guttural with troubled breath,
Shrouded in a rumpled coverlet.

Rubbing the sleep from your eyes,
You will smile at me with real affection,
But I will not see it.

Soon, you will be percolating grounds
As though you lived here.

You and I and he will sit together at his table,
Passing the sugar, passing the milk.
Scrambled eggs and sausage meat.

But tonight, we are on our way out.
You hold the gate open for me.
You leave it, swinging, behind you.

The Passenger

You watch her as she skips across the patio;
Lies face down on a towel by the pool;
Leaps up, jumps in, gets out again
Before a length; lies wet, the light
Invested in each droplet on her back.

★

I watch her concentration in reverse
I notice you, between your seats, the clutch:
Your fingers tremble on her thigh until
She grips them, lets them go and takes
A firmer handle on the wheel.

★

While waiting for our flight to leave
You take a postcard out and write.
*L'Amour reanimated with the kiss
Of Psyche,* hallmarked by your own.

★

An hour after take-off, you are still,
Embedding your impressions on a pad,
Laying down discoveries for future archaeologists,
Tracing her evaporated shade.

Rain

Once, after a bout of heavy rain,
I walked the streets of Paris for the kick
Of catching lovers kissing in their doors—
There were none that I could find.

    Maybe, in this town, the act of kissing
    Cloaks you in a shade of grain and glass.

I searched for clues. A woman,
Testing perfumes in Samaritaine,
Hovered over atomised chrysanthemums,
Then walked into a cloud, the ghostly
Molecules attracting still, though flowers
And their bees were long deceased.

    Maybe, in this town, the act of dying
    Cloaks you in a shade of love and scent.

Outside, a pregnant woman
With a pit bull like a ball-and-chain
Gave her dog a toilet break
Upon a sapling pushing through the stone,
Then tugged on him, as though he were
A human child, and dog-piss, lemonade.

    Maybe in this town the act of loving
    Cloaks you in a shade of hope and pain.

An old man wearing better clothes than mine,
Appearing casually spiritual
And godless in the same small frown,
Watched a younger man and woman
Intimate their mutual claim

With hands dug deep inside each other's
Pockets as they promenaded.

    Maybe, in this town, the act of yearning
    Cloaks you in a shade of blues and death.

The cinemas in Montparnasse
Were showing English-language tales
Of love in the original
American. I did not feel
Like following the titles—so
I went in search of raindrops
Still intact upon the paving stones.

    Maybe, in this town, the act of falling
    Cloaks you in a shade of air and speed.

Part Five

Eidolon

Years go by and all your loves devolve into a composite,
Passing on time's travelator, gliding to a terminal,
Never to be seen again and you watch from Security,
Frisked as though this stood for sex, this stood for *intimate*.

Ghosts—and you are ignorant of exorcism rites.
Whenever you're entangled in some temporary angel
Comes the shadow of another love: a flicker of a dimple
Or the first arrested syllable of laughter soft as promises.

You meet her in Departures after half a decade lost
And it's no longer her but her extrapolated. Someone
Calls her over—time to make the plane—and flings
A prophylactic glance at you, you melancholy revenant.

The Lost Planet

In the blue room, he saw his wife.
She sat up in the bed and drew
The sheet around her shoulders.
Her elbows were spiked like breast plates.

In the white room, he saw himself,
Asking her if everything
That came before this moment
Was scripted to lead up to it—
And all that happened afterwards,
Designed to lead him away.

In the red room, he saw his wife.
With kindness, she reached out to him.
She took his forehead in her hands.
She kissed it, told him not to fret.
She guided him inside herself.
She felt connectedness.

In the black room, he saw himself.
Momentum loosed a fleet of probes
That lit their launching tower
And set out to reclaim for her
A planet lost to him once found—
But each contraction struck him
With a flashback to the future:

He evolves into the pupal stage
Of woman-baby butterfly.

Storing Dreams

I remember your dreams:
Naked in public, being dead,
Teeth falling out, being chased.

I hold them in my fingernail
For you to gather later,
When your sleep has room for them.

Cicatrice

You did not see mine, on the first night we met.
You were occupied, putting your hand
Through my window, not feeling the pain,
Bleeding your wrist on invisible shards
As you opened the frame just a crack for some air,
Letting autumn leaves in from the fingers of trees.
At some point, we made love, or a bungled attempt.
By the morning, your blood had congealed.

Wounded and practical, no broken bird,
You tried often to show me how two falling leaves
Might collide in the rain, on a current, and sail
As one leaf. In the end, winter rattled us loose.
Now and then, subtle scars raise a sign on my skin
That you left more in me than I ever let on.

West Winter Street

October cloud dissolving black—
Glaucoma night becoming blind.
Behind it, sky was ocean—

Moon became a weathervane,
Tethered to the bed by cables:
Silver, braided moonlight. Down

Below my tired lover told of Hopi
Women, in seclusion, in the moon time:
Visitations, debts of passion; apparitions

As substantial as a Brave or soil or buffalo.
Meeting with the redcoats, they
Brought visions to the shaman.

Soon she drowsed. The clouds had left
A violet sky, a cowl for coming
Moon time in the world. I kissed

Her lips goodnight and slithered out
From underneath our eiderdown,
A subtle tang of iron on my tongue.

Tunisia, Winter 1998

For Yvonne

Tonight, in moonlight, your pellucid skin
Is gleaming as a silent-movie star's,
Open lips caressed by playful rays.
Between the jet-black comma of your hair
And the Berber blanket's fringe
That frame your beautiful face like a still—
Your complexion is so clear as to be luminous
As moonlight itself on the crown of a nimbus.

In weeks, all we'll have of each other is desert—
A couple of jars filled with camel-ride sand.
Now, I watch over your dreaming—secure
For the moment, unsleeping but drowsy,
My bare arm exposed at the edge of the bed
That is furthest away from your body:
By the time the mosquito—proboscis drawn in—
Is aware of your breath, she'll have taken her fill.